The Earned Lifestyle:

Choose Satisfaction Instead of Regret.

Katherina C. Norton

Table of Contents

Chapter 1

What's stopping you from creating your own life

According to studies, one of the most often used justifications for excuses is a failure. Another near the top of the list is fear of the unknown. Whatever your justification, remember that if you keep coming up with them, you'll never achieve your goals. Instead, begin developing solutions. Here is an explanation for each day of the month and a response to each one.

1. I'm pressed for time

Making the time is the answer. If you don't make the time, you won't make a strategy to accomplish your goals. Begin modestly. Consider your week. Consider if you have two hours to spare. You can do it across six days in 20-minute intervals while still taking one day off. For 20 minutes each day, work toward your goal. That is much superior to having no time at all.

Utilize a project management app like Trello to organize your chores into projects and balance your priorities. Children, challenging work, a difficult commute, a full social life, and several tasks to manage? It is irrelevant. There is a way if you have the will. You discover you can stop wasting time by watching TV, using your smartphone to browse the web, and sending pals texts after taking a broad picture of your week and starting to drill down to each day.

The moment is now.

I'm too young, 2.
The answer: Mozart began writing music at the age of five and performed for royal audiences. Heck, my three-year-old kid, who just started a baseball league, will do it next weekend! Being "too young" should never, ever be a deterrent for someone who wants to begin living their dream or continue living it.

All you need to write for Medium is an email address. no age restriction. Develop a passion for reading. Nothing can stop you from accessing the Internet or books at your local library once you learn to read. People who claim you are too young are also those who wish to keep you in your place so they may continue to be in positions of authority and control. Set your path and defy them.

3. I'm becoming old
Solution: Let me share with you a few historical figures who, despite being considered "ancient," performed amazing feats:

The Cat in the Hat was written by Dr. Seuss, whose birthday is today when he was 54 years old.

The best work Alfred Hitchcock ever produced was in his 50s and 60s.

In his later years, Cezanne produced some of his greatest works of art.

You may start living the life you desire at any time. Do you need extra motivation? Read Late Bloomers by Malcolm Gladwell. Your life could be affected.

4. I lack sufficient funds
Who is to claim that you need money? Many of the most well-known business giants of our time—including Oprah Winfrey, Gordon Ramsey, LeBron James, and many others—came from extremely humble beginnings. These individuals had little chance of success as children. Do those who are wealthy have better access and advantages? Undoubtedly, sure.

For those of us who weren't given all we ever wanted, the fire, nonetheless, burns brighter. To get the funding required to enact change and improve people's lives, we must exert more effort. Between now and then, we have access to the Internet, literature, affordable transportation, and a limitless number of creative opportunities. If you can't succeed without money, you probably won't succeed with money either.

5. Nobody cares about what I have to say.
Solution: Develop a more critical mindset. Read more, watch YouTube videos, and explore your community to learn about its culture. Become an authority in a subject that you are passionate about and that you are aware other people are as well. Everyone will suddenly be interested in hearing what the assured, knowledgeable lady or guy has to say about social media, healthcare, digital marketing, etc.

6. I won't succeed
Start thinking more optimistically as a solution. This justification is the definition of pessimism. Thinking negatively breeds prejudice, skepticism, and fear. Watch YouTube's inspiring lectures. On Leadercast

or Goalcast, you may find lectures that promote optimism. Spend time with successful people who will inspire you and give you hope. Create a life based on your ideals and seek out motivating people to assist you to go forward.

7. I lack the necessary connections
Solution: Having that wealthy uncle who can open the doors to that record executive's office would undoubtedly make things simpler, wouldn't it? Guess what, though? Most likely, you don't own it. Connect the dots! Join Linkedin and start corresponding with professionals and wealthy businesspeople who could be willing to help you. Most likely, they won't reply. But some will. Request only 30 minutes of those people's time to meet up for a cup of coffee so you may absorb all of their knowledge and experience like a sponge.

If you want to learn something new, get in touch with authors like myself on Medium and be personable and open to getting in touch with others.

8. I never get a break

Retry is the answer. once again. once again. once again. You get the picture, right? One of the keys to success is persistence. One of two factors is likely the case if "luck" isn't on your side or you haven't exactly achieved success in what you've tried: You have two options: either you need to keep trying and moving forward, or it could be time to shift directions and attempt something new that you won't give up on.

Spend some time evaluating what you're working on honestly. It could include looking for a partner or girlfriend. It could include aspiring to be a singer, writer, or businessperson. Create a strategy, put your trust behind it, and go ahead until you achieve your goals.

9. I'm not sure how to proceed.

Solution: Stop what you're doing, please. Visit Google and type the following into the search bar to find what you're searching for: How to. Find the greatest links and articles. I can almost ensure that someone has previously thought of a method to do what you want to achieve.

10. My education is insufficient
Solution: Since when is success determined by having "enough" education? Jennifer Lawrence only completed middle school. Bill Gates quit his studies at Harvard. Are these unusual tales? Yes, but it's not inconceivable. In many cases, continuing your education in a secondary school or a university is the best course of action. However, it's not the only option.

You may now self-educate using a wealth of materials, many of which are free. Become absorbed in learning. If you maintain your education throughout your life, regardless of whether you attend college or specialize in a certain area, you will be in excellent condition.

When you recognize that everything that occurs in life is a product of the past decisions you made and begin making new choices to improve your life, you have reached maturity.

Roger T. Bennett

11. I lack the necessary skill
Solution: Keep in mind this basketball coaching proverb. While coaching at the high school level, I discovered that talent is only superior to hard work when talent puts in the effort.

To put it another way, having a positive outlook and a motivated, diligent work ethic can help you achieve your goals in life. What's best? Both are entirely in your hands.

12. No one is interested in me. (art, work, writing, business, etc.)
Find the correct audience as a solution. Apply Medium. Utilize social media sites such as Instagram, Snapchat, Linkedin, Facebook, Twitter, YouTube, and others to promote your amazing work. Find a mentor, teacher, coach, or school official who will show you attention if your friends, coworkers, and family do not. If you're lucky, take advantage of community activities like the YMCA or Boys & Girls Club.

Never let fear rule your life. Don't think your daring ideas or you are unimportant. You are exceptional and extraordinary, and you have something amazing to offer the world. Be open-minded and willing to try new things. You may have to look for a long, but you'll eventually discover someone who wants to help.

My parents tell me I can't do it.

Solution: Find out why your parents are preventing you from doing what you enjoy by asking them. Don't be a victim of the limited thinking of others, even your parents. Never let the opinions of those closest to you deter you from achieving your goals if you have faith in your ability to do so. Tell them how and why you are confident in your abilities.

Accept it for what it is and keep going if they still won't listen. Sometimes in life, our deepest desires are known only to ourselves. Even our parents could attempt to prevent us from achieving our potential. Maybe they didn't get to do what they wanted to accomplish. Never allow their unpleasant experiences to influence you. You simply need to satisfy your standards.

14. My pals don't think I can pull this off.
Solution: See item 13 above. You could be socializing with the wrong people. Maybe all you need to do is tell your pals about your

vision, your objectives, and how you intend to get what you desire. Speaking and visualizing what you want can help you get the agreement you need to convince yourself that you are doing appropriately.

15. I'm exhausted

Solution: If you're always exhausted, you may need to see a doctor find the source of your fatigue. In the unlikely event that this isn't the case, there's a strong likelihood that you don't have enough things in your life to motivate, inspire, and ignite your enthusiasm. Start engaging in activities you like that are productive, uplifting, and have a beneficial impact on both you and others.

Learn more about something that ignites a fire within of you and get hooked to the sense of assisting others. Then, assess your level of fatigue.

16. I lack access to the necessary technologies

Solution: Even if you can't afford a 4K TV or a very costly camera, you probably have access to the internet. That means you have access to some of the greatest musical recordings ever made, the best books ever written, the best pieces of art ever created, and the inventors, artists, and entrepreneurs who have shaped the world around you. Free of charge.

17. I don't own a vehicle
Solution: If you reside in a large city where public transit is unquestionably your best option, this is less of a problem. But suppose you reside in a rural area or another location where a vehicle is considerably more useful for traveling about. There's Uber, of course. Spend your savings on a bicycle. instead, rent one. Take a walk, jog, or bike with a buddy. Find a means to get to where you need to be physical.

19. I'm too timid

I used to be quite bashful, too. By surrounding myself with individuals who made me realize that "sitting on the sidelines" was the surest way to lose out on all the abundant, magnificent things life had to offer, I was able to overcome my anxiety. The game of life is contact. To lead the life you want, you must participate in the game. You must overcome fear or shyness to place yourself in a position to achieve your goals, whether it be pursuing a romantic interest, developing an idea, or applying for a job you believe is out of your league.

19. I'm shy and uncomfortable in front of others.
Solution: If speaking in front of a group or public is not your thing, concentrate on employment that enables you to work alone. In the comfort of your apartment, you may rise to fame as a blogger. Just a computer and an Internet connection are required. Many technological tasks may be completed with little or no contact with others.

However, you'll ultimately have to collaborate with others. In our interconnected world, decisions are made in concert with other people's thoughts and behaviors. Develop your speaking in front of an audience. Confidently consider your capabilities. Imagine communicating with people in your mind's eye. When no one is watching, practice at home. It's not necessary to be outgoing. Introverts often have great success.

20. My worst critic is myself

Solution: Okay, time for a confession: I think this is the one I used the most often. Heck, I still do it sometimes. I'm pretty hard on myself, and I often feel like I've accomplished nothing when I see others' accomplishments. I have to keep my victories in mind. I take a look at my five-year plan and count how many goals I've accomplished.

It's crucial to keep in mind that this defense may work both as a gift and a curse. I advise you to set high standards for yourself but to also be practical and take care of yourself. Speak positive affirmations over your life and encourage yourself. They'll block out the bad ideas and assist you in overcoming damaging self-criticism.

The problem with excuses is that once they have been used a few times, it is impossible to believe them anymore.

Mr. Scott Spencer

I'm unsure of what I want.
Solution: I often hear this one from folks who are miserable, aimless, and always in the same area. I have the following really easy workout for you: Get a pen and paper, then sit down. Make a running list of all the things that make you happy, motivate you, ignite your passion, and promote positive thinking.

You might discover that you love to serve others by doing something as easy as reflecting on your affection for children. Perhaps engaging in coaching or teaching can bring you happiness. Even just writing is calming and beneficial. Launch a daily diary. Continue listing the things you like. You'll soon have a list of endeavors to pursue. After that, all that remains is for you to act.

22. I am aware of what I desire, yet I am unable to get it

Solution: Start copying successful individuals who have already accomplished what you want to achieve. Read on to find out how they managed to reach their goals. How do you become a superb guitarist? What are the requirements for launching a profitable internet business? In the meanwhile, keep going for what you want as you start looking into how to get there.

23. I am unable to locate a mentor or supporter.

Solution: Through the Small Business Administration, the US federal government provides SCORE, a free program. Click on this link to see them. You can discover a ton of materials on their website alone if you're looking to improve your company. Meeting someone who has "been there, done that" in person is where you go to win.

Look nearby. Start by talking to your loved ones, instructors, coaches, or others who are already doing what you want to do well online. Again, you'll never know if you never give it a go.

24. No one from where I originate from "makes it out" or "has ever done anything"

Never cite your geography or place of origin as a justification. It is dumb, ineffective, and lazy. Create your specialty and be motivated by your desire to be a "hometown hero." If your surroundings are restricting your creativity and inspiration, you may need to relocate or go to a different location.

It can be more difficult for you to leave where you are since you come from a harsh area. Prioritize your safety and have faith in your loving family and friends. Maintain your composure and educate yourself on what it will take to succeed via education, internship opportunities, or community-based initiatives.

History does not accept the justification of difficulty.

– Ed. R. Murrow

I'll never be able to kick this habit.
Solution: Instead of succumbing to addiction, look at the underlying reasons why you can't quit doing something that isn't beneficial to you. How did this behavior begin? How can you ask for assistance from

friends or internet resources to navigate your way to the other side?

One of the most important life lessons I've discovered is that for people to assist us, we must be willing to accept assistance. Allow someone to aid you. Don't be arrogant. Be not scared. Open up, own your need for assistance, and learn how to break your habit in a mature, responsible manner. The bravest thing you will ever do is to ask for assistance.

I'll never meet the ideal person for me, number 26.
Solution: Surround yourself with things you like doing and opportunities to accomplish them. The greatest method to find the "perfect" person for you is to become involved in something that makes you feel your best. Get engaged in coaching a sport or go to a game of the team you support if you enjoy basketball.

If serving others and helping others is your calling, volunteer your time for a cause in your neighborhood, such as looking after the elderly or working at a children's hospital. Who you'll run into is always a mystery. Possibly someone seeking someone similar to you.

27. My looks are preventing me from moving forward
Solution: You're thinking about things incorrectly if you believe that your appearance, weight, or any other flaw is what's bothering you. The only thing that matters is who you are on the inside. If you believe that your look is detracting from your work, consider what it could take to reduce weight. Improve your self-care by working out or dressing differently.

Think about going back to #20 as well. You could be too hard on yourself. You typically have control over your diet, or what you consume. To have a healthy lifestyle, do some research. Find dependable individuals who will hold you responsible and motivate you to keep working toward your objectives.

28. I continue to make the same errors
Solution: Establish a method where you record your errors or failures in an electronic diary or planner. To encourage you in the morning, look at them every day. Put a reminder in your Outlook, Evernote, or another app to remind you of this during the week, for instance, if your error was neglecting to send out a report at work.

We are all far better off for having made errors, but it's preferable to limit them to occasional slip-ups. Take lessons from the hardship. Decide how to keep yourself responsible when you commit, plan your time effectively, and guarantee that you fully commit to completing the work at hand. Make it your personal goal to rectify errors to erase them.

29. I can't achieve this on my Solution: We all need assistance to realize our greatest ambitions, but much of the beginning is up to you. When you refuse to identify some of the core tenets of your existence, you cannot blame others:

Values

The Meaning of Success

Success Indicators

Goals

Key Results

Consider your values first. I have such a strong conviction in this that I developed a book on selecting and pursuing our essential beliefs. Both the process of identifying my values and the drafting of the book greatly altered my life and assisted me in setting priorities based on what is most important to me. Beginning with these actions and working diligently to fulfill your goals, you'll discover that you get the assistance you need along the road.

30. It's what everyone else is doing
Solution: Let's go. Accept responsibility for yourself and concentrate on your sphere of influence and control. Stop assigning blame or making excuses for others. Run your race!

Chapter 2

The Art of asking for Help

Have you ever wondered where the term "mayday," the global distress signal used by ships and airplanes, came from? In the introduction of her latest book, Mayday! M. Nora Klaver, a master coach located in Chicago, notes in her book Asking for Help in Times of Need (Berrett-Koehler, 2007): "It derives from the French m'aidez (pronounced similarly to the term mayday) and translates to 'help me.'" According to Klaver, the phrase is sometimes employed in daily life by persons who have crossed their particular threshold of terror or despair.

Do you put off asking for assistance until it's really necessary? It's not just you. In her book, Klaver outlines a few of the reasons why individuals often wait until they are in a desperate situation before making a legitimate request for assistance. She says:

We could wait too long to ask because we fail to acknowledge our need for something too soon.

The assistance we requested could only have partially met our needs since we couldn't see the complete picture.

We can approach the incorrect individual or individuals with our request.

Others may not grasp that we even need aid because of how vague our demands might be.

Aid could arrive, but it won't be the right help since we weren't specific enough in our inquiries.

Instead of asking for help respectfully, we can demand it.

To satisfy our demands, we could use compulsion, blackmail, or even bribery.

We could unintentionally ask for sympathy rather than support.

Our bodies may reveal our concerns and discreetly suggest that we are beyond saving.

Without regard for our friends, family, and colleagues, we could seek assistance much too often. For them, compassion fatigue becomes a genuine possibility.

We could just scare ourselves out of asking.

The good news, according to Klaver, is that you can learn to ask for assistance. In actuality, it can be a rather easy deed. But first, you need to dispel certain widely held cultural misconceptions. For instance:

Myth: Seeking assistance makes you seem weak or dependent.

In actuality, there is no shame in asking for help when you need it. In actuality, it's a show of power.

Myth: Seeking assistance makes you seem weak or dependent.

In actuality, there is no shame in asking for help when you need it. In actuality, it's a show of power.

Myth: Seeking assistance implies ineptitude, particularly at work.
Reality: Asking for assistance at work demonstrates to others your desire to perform the job well as well as to grow and learn.

Myth: Seeking assistance may damage relationships.
Reality: Healthy relationships include giving as well as receiving, not just giving.

Myth: Asking for assistance makes people uncomfortable.
Reality: When you see someone in need, it's human nature to assist; the same holds when other people see you in need.

Myth: Requesting assistance may result in rejection.
Reality: Every answer, even a "no," is a chance to discover new things about you and your relationships.

Myth: By seeking assistance, the task may not be completed properly.

Reality: Refusing to inquire out of a sense of controllessness keeps things as they are. Allow your helper to succeed by letting go.

Myth: You have to give back if you ask for assistance.

Reality: There are no conditions placed on free assistance other than a straightforward and heartfelt thank you.

Myth: Asking for aid just isn't done in the United States.

Reality: Success comes from excellent traits like independence and self-sufficiency. But the foundation of any successful organization, including our own country, is support, cooperation, and teamwork.

A Mayday! Process

Klaver suggests a seven-step process to make sure your mayday signals are sent with both intensity and clarity:

What is the need? Asking yourself these questions can help you take your time and determine precisely what you need. Avoid being too wedded to your first theory regarding how to handle the circumstance.
Take a break for yourself. Unless you feel you deserve it, you will never be able to ask for assistance openly.
Go for a jump. You must possess the self-assurance required to take a leap of faith in the direction of the assistance you want.
Ask! The request is made at this stage. Increase the number of people on your list of helpmates; come up with as many possible helpers as you can, even if they may decline.

Being thankful An essential component of the process is gratitude. It enables you to maintain your composure and openness whatever the outcome of your request.

Adapt your listening. When someone responds to your request, pay attention to the underlying emotional cues as well as the words they use.

Thank you. Whether your helpmate accepts your offer or not, the last step is to express your gratitude. By expressing your appreciation three times—when the deal is made, when the need is satisfied, and when you next encounter your helper—you are following the "three thanks" rule.

Even to those who are most reluctant to seek assistance, Klaver brings inspiration and optimism. Like any talent, practice is necessary, the author says. You will feel more at ease if you inquire more often. Miscommunications will become less often, tension will subside, and your language will improve with time.

Chapter 3

The Building blocks of Discipline

Regarding the need for discipline, there is very little disagreement, and I have studied so many personal development theories that I have lost track. Depending on the author's area of expertise, target audience, and objective, each one varies. There are no bad tools, but certain instruments could be more effective in a specific context than others, has always been my stance. The discipline of some kind is the one element that is always present in a good development paradigm. Unfortunately, since every model defines discipline differently, anytime we attempt to speak about it, we often find ourselves drowning in subtlety and terminology. Although these existential discussions have their place, they are seldom useful in our daily lives.

Let's talk about what I think are the three most important elements of discipline:

intentionality, consistency, and attention to detail. Being a better man doesn't take a Ph.D. I have discovered that the framework provided by these three ideas can solve roughly 90% of the discipline-related queries I get. Move it!

Intentionality

Nothing you do is an accident when you operate with an intentional attitude because everything you do has a purpose. We leave the luxury of "flowing with the flow" to our children since as males, we are unable to do so. Instead, we constantly consider the causes and outcomes of our decisions. We always put our whole effort into everything we do, and we never entrust the results of our efforts to anybody else. Because they seldom go unprepared, men who live intentionally are damned-near resistant to victimization, even when things don't go as planned. A guy cannot ensure that he won't run into difficulties like a flat tire, no matter how careful he is, but he knows that his spare tire and jack are in good shape, and he understands how to use them if necessary. He won't have to worry about obtaining a flat tire as a result. He can manage what is within his power and reduce what is beyond his control by acting with purpose.

In a practical sense, intentionality puts us in control. Whatever position we find ourselves in—good, horrible, or neutral—we drove ourselves there. This kind of ownership is both difficult and empowering, as I explored last week. On the one hand, if anything in your life is going wrong, the only person to blame is you. On the other hand, if you are solely responsible for your circumstances, you have complete control over them.

Be purposeful.

Consistency

Consistency is a dependable pattern that has persisted throughout time. This is the most difficult of the three parts for almost every one of us. Consistency is the main component of trust, thus it may also have the greatest influence. The general idea of trust is as follows, but I'll write more about it next week:

We gain the confidence of people by maintaining our consistency throughout time.

Consider the employee at your workplace who always arrives on time and performs top-notch work. His manager will often have more faith in him if he is consistent like that. Liken him to the unreliable employee who often shows up late and performs poorly. Consistency always pays well when it comes time to promote someone.

Think about how much your spouse or children trust you and how consistent you are with them. Safety is the priority for the majority of women and all children. Your regularity in these interactions fosters security and trust. We react differently to others when we are impulsive or moody.

Pro-Tip: If you've been erratic in your actions, emotions, or behaviors, your spouse or kids may be scared to break unpleasant news to you. They shouldn't be subjected to any nasty surprises, not from you.

Being consistent requires playing the long game, which is difficult to do. It requires time. Even after your tenth exercise, you won't notice results, but if we are committed to being consistent, the results will appear. On the other hand, consistency gets more ingrained in our personality the longer we practice it.

Be dependable.

Details

The foundation of a disciplined man details. This one will be simple for you if you have a little obsessive behavior as I do. You'll need to put forth some effort if not. There are two causes to pay attention to the specifics:

Details are crucial at the beginning. Any military veteran can attest to the value of paying close attention to detail. The cornerstones of a disciplined squad were a neat, crisp uniform, a haircut, and shiny boots. None of these norms by themselves are sufficient to win the conflict; rather, they form the cornerstone of the disciplined mentality that counts when the stakes go beyond one's outward appearance. A malfunctioning weapon or missing piece of essential equipment might have tragic consequences.

Your message to them is included in those specifics. They take note of your arrival time when you have an appointment. When someone enters your vehicle or truck, they can immediately tell how well you maintain your machinery. Consider your word choice and language more carefully while communicating if you want others to take you seriously. Organize and keep your desk clean. Spending a few additional seconds to perfect your look might leave a lasting impression of your attention to detail.

When a guy doesn't give enough consideration to the little things:

He's ironing his shirt

arriving on time

taking good care of his tools (and his body)

or even finishing a statement with a period,

Others worry about what else he may not care about because of him.

Be mindful of the little things.

Chapter 4

Make Earning an habit

Money is perhaps the most taboo subject in society after sex.

People seldom discuss their financial situation, including how much they earn and maintain.

And as a result, when the children become 18 or 21, they are suddenly expected to manage their finances.

I experienced the same thing.

At the age of 20, I was suddenly responsible for managing my funds.

I have learned money-making and money-keeping techniques from industry gurus throughout the years.

Continue reading if you want to create simple daily routines that will help you earn and retain more money. I'm writing this for you.

Habit 1: Express gratitude each time you put or take money out of your wallet.
I got this tip straight from Vishen, a co-founder of Mindvalley.

I've been engaging in this behavior for the last four months, and dammit! Magic exists here!

Close your eyes for a minute and express thanks for the money anytime you pay someone, even for a coffee, or whenever you get any payment or paycheck.

When you give someone money, remember to express your gratitude for being in a position to do so.

Since money is unquestionably a useful resource. Furthermore, you express thanks to the universe for using you as the source to provide this gift to others.

When you get any money, be thankful for the ability it gives you to change so many lives.

Feel blessed that the universe provided you with such a powerful tool.

Warning: This method is magical. After this, be careful not to feel "too good" about your finances.

Habit 2: Create a budget, either daily or monthly.

And you don't have to focus on the smallest things... Simply make sure you have a rough sense of how much money you are generating and spending.

You shouldn't if you just have one source of income. Work on expanding your revenue streams.

In any case, if you just had one source of income, you would know roughly how much you are making.

This type becomes necessary if you're self-employed and have various sources of income.

You might try keeping track of your costs on a daily, weekly, or monthly basis.

For this, I'm using Google Sheet. You may also give a notepad a go.

Travel, rent, and
Friend-making, Groceries
Some people
Habit 3: List your financial objectives
Set financial objectives for the next month, three months, year, and five years.

Determine how much you want your account to be worth after five years.

Consider your insurance, any unforeseen family situations, your family's needs, any debts, and the vehicles you wish to drive.

Practice this one habit once a week. This will help you to clearly define your financial objectives.

And engaging in this action would be equivalent to making a written request to the cosmos.

You will begin searching for methods to make it happen if you are sure that you want to earn X by 2025. if not, your aspirations will just ever be that.

The first step in making your aspirations a reality is to put your objectives on paper.

Habit 4: Affirmations of plenty
I sometimes use this 8-hour audio to fall asleep. Try it; it's fantastic!

Say several affirmations, such as:

I draw money to myself.
I am entitled to financial success.
Everything I need is freely provided for by the cosmos.
My world is one of plenty and peace.
Even when I'm sleeping, money flows to me freely and readily.
Avalanches of money come to me in abundance.
I'm glad to have money plenty in my life right now.
My life is filled with wealth.
And there are so many more inspirational statements.

When we adopt an abundant attitude, we start coming up with new business ideas. Or the cosmos begins to provide in other ways.

Habit 5: Research finances
This should be obvious, right?

One of the greatest in the field is Ramit Sethi. He taught me a lot about managing my own money.

His idea of "defining your rich life" completely altered my perspective.

You're asked by Ramit Sethi to describe your wonderful existence. Decide what in your life pleases you. Spend the money without hesitation on such things.

Additionally, list all the things in your life that bring you no pleasure, then ruthlessly reduce your consumption of those things.

For me, buying books cost a lot of money. I ADORE reading. And I seldom give a book a second thought before buying it.

On the other side, I don't often purchase many pairs of shoes or clothing. Good, good, good.

What do you LOVE to buy with money?

Talk to your friend, habit no. 6
Talk about money. Make it a frequent subject of discussion.

At first, there can be some jealousy there, but you need to go beyond it.

Share everything that you are aware of about earning and maintaining money.

Find out from them how they earn and manage their money.

The first time Anangsha Alammyan and I discussed our earnings and sources of revenue, I still clearly recall how unpleasant it was.

She expressed to me her desire to increase her writing income. We, therefore, spoke about her alternatives.

I saw a few financial barriers in her consciousness and helped her go through them.

What is the outcome?

Five months after we originally discussed this, she is now making three times as much money from her work.

This leads me to my next point.

Habit 7: Get Rid of Your Financial Blocks
Money blockages are fundamental assumptions that prevent you from achieving your financial goals.

Here is a basic explanation of the differences between plentiful and restricted money ideas.

Having humble beginnings and seeing my parents sacrifice much for my schooling... I've always thought that making money took a lot of time and work.

I began being paid much more than I had expected over time as I consistently accomplished things that came naturally to me.

I love money, but I wasn't taking the money that was coming my way because of the money barrier "Money takes time and work."

This limiting notion was identified by my coach, and we worked on it.

What did I start to believe now?

"When you do what comes naturally to you, money flows easily to you."

The hardest aspect of money blocks, do you know?

We can seldom ever find our financial hurdles. Help is needed.

We need assistance in identifying our financial blocks.

What should you do to address your limiting beliefs?

Employ a coach. Request assistance.

Chapter 5

Power of Productive Routines

Words like monotonous or commonplace may come to mind when you hear the term "routine". Routines may have seemed monotonous and constrictive during the pandemic's disturbances to everyday life. But as an occupational therapist who studies the effects of involvement and exercise on mental health, I am aware that routines may be effective strategies. They may promote health, assist cognitive function, and provide chances for meaningful activities and social interaction.

Early on in the epidemic, researchers emphasized the importance of routines in preparing for change. Reflecting on routines and their worth is helpful while moving toward a "new normal" as the second anniversary of the epidemic coincides with the easing of public health measures across.

Routines help cognitive process

First of all, a regular schedule and habits may help individuals think more clearly and even free them up to be more creative. According to research, having routine work procedures enables employees to use less mental energy on repetitive activities, which may enhance concentration and creativity for more challenging jobs.

Consider the normal morning activities that took place before the pandemic: assisting family members with their travel, taking a familiar route to work, stopping for a warm beverage along the way, introducing oneself to colleagues, turning on a computer, or opening a calendar. Such routines may pave the way for an effective workday.

When prominent artists' daily routines were examined, it was discovered that many of them had established work habits that may encourage rather than limit their creativity.

According to a memory study, routines and habits might help older people perform better in their homes.

It will take less effort to seek lost items and worry about preserving one's health if taking prescriptions at the same time as putting the keys away is part of a regular habit, freeing up time for other things individuals want to accomplish in their day.

Regularity fosters wellness
Regular routines may also provide individuals with a sense of control over their day-to-day life and the ability to manage their health. For instance, scheduling exercise into routines may assist in achieving required daily activity levels. This is particularly important right now since studies indicate that persons who decreased their exercise levels during the epidemic may have suffered long-term health impacts.

As individuals become more active outside of their houses, they may think about using public transportation to work and school, going back to organized exercise activities, going to the gym, and finding chances to move throughout the day. Regularly preparing meals and getting adequate sleep are two other ways that routines may promote health. These actions may seem easy, but they can have a lasting positive impact on aging healthily.

Routines give life to things.
Regular routines may enhance life by adding some variety in addition to simplifying everyday duties. There is evidence that a healthy exercise like walking may provide opportunities to appreciate nature, discover new areas, and interact with others.

Sports, games, the arts, and music, according to research on the notion of flow, a state of complete immersion in the present moment, maybe gratifying and supportive.

Regular engagement in worthwhile and enjoyable activities may also benefit mental health.

Little by little, establish habits
If you believe that your everyday routines may need some improvement, use these simple measures:

• To plan your activities and include the things you wish to accomplish in your calendar, use a daytimer or a smartphone app.

• Establish a regular wake-up and bedtime, and make an effort to adhere to it most days of the week.

• Make exercise manageable by going for a couple of weekly neighborhood walks or bike rides.

• Take up a new interest or pick up an old one again, such as singing, playing an instrument, producing crafts, participating in sports, or playing video games.

• Keep a look out for worthwhile endeavors that could be resurfacing in your neighborhood, such as a reading club at the library or a group for social strolling.

We may manage our health, as well as our life at work, home, and in the community, with the use of routines. People now have the chance to think about the routines they want to preserve and the significant items they need in their daily lives to be productive, happy, and healthy two years after the epidemic impacted everyone's life.

Chapter 6

Paying the price of Eating the Frog

The practices that helped the most successful individuals get where they now include being more cheerful and productive. These behaviors position children for greater success in life.

And one of the most crucial habits I've picked up along the way, something I think of as a hidden weapon, is eating frogs.

While I recognize it initially seems a little unusual, allow me to clarify what I mean and precisely how to "eat that frog" for you to reach your objectives and lead the ideal possible existence.

Your "frog" is your greatest and most crucial responsibility. If you don't take action, it will be the one you put off doing the most.

So, "eat that frog" is another way of stating to start with the largest, toughest, and most essential duty first if you have two vital chores to do.

Set boundaries for yourself so that you may start right away and keep going until the work is finished before moving on to anything else.

Getting That Frog to Eat
Creating the lifetime habit of starting your primary activity each morning is the key to achieving high levels of performance and productivity. You need to get into the habit of "eating your frog" without thinking about it too much and before you do anything else.

This behavior is common among successful individuals, so much so that I think it is a necessary leadership trait for anybody hoping to achieve great things.

Here's how to "eat that frog" in the most enjoyable manner possible now that you understand what a "frog" is and how to recognize one.

Decide to Be Positive
Your body responds by sending endorphins to your brain when you have pleasant memories, ideas, or emotions. Endorphins give you a positive, contented feeling.

Endorphins and the sensation of increased clarity, self-assurance, and competence they provide may become physically addictive.

You start to get used to having a cheerful outlook quite quickly. Unconsciously, you'll start to arrange your life such that you're consistently beginning and finishing ever-more significant jobs and projects. You will develop an addiction to achievement and service in a very good sense, which will enable you to "eat that frog" in the most enjoyable manner imaginable.

You may get this "hooked" sensation by setting both short- and long-term SMART objectives. The brain's reward and pleasure systems are activated by the gratification of completing each task.

Put an end to seeking shortcuts.
Long-term success cannot be attained quickly.

No matter how many blogs, YouTube videos, or podcasts you read, watch, or listen to in an attempt to discover a faster route to success, significant victories go to those who are patient and invest the time to become a master.

Any talent may be mastered with enough practice. Thankfully, your mind is flexible like a muscle. With usage, it becomes stronger and more effective. Any behavior or habit that you deem to be either good or essential may be learned with practice.

Once you make the effort to consume that frog, you can also quickly come to prefer doing your most important tasks first and promptly. The benefits are satisfying in every way!

One frog at a time, please
This is another way of expressing that you should start with the largest, toughest, and more essential job first if you have two critical chores to do.

When you attempt to bite off more than you can chew, things get overwhelming, and you are unable to continue working or eating the frog.

The main idea of eating a frog is to concentrate on one major work at a time, even though it may be exhilarating to complete large chores and useful to plan.

To succeed in life, have the discipline to get started right away and to stick with it until the work is finished before moving on to anything else.

Do Something
Individuals that jump right into their important responsibilities and then discipline themselves to work consistently and single-mindedly until those tasks are completed are successful, productive people.

One of the major issues facing companies today is execution. However, a lot of people equate exercise with success. They conduct many meetings, chat nonstop, and create fantastic ideas, but nobody gets the work done or produces the outcomes that are needed in the end.

For instance, unless your want is transformed from a desire into a goal, you won't be able to develop your profession, expand your company, or enhance the lives of others by becoming a published author, for example. You still need to take action and begin writing right away to be successful even at that moment.

Only when you eventually put your ideas into action, establish the objective, and learn how to write a book will your dream and all of those potential advantages be able to provide long-lasting results.

The same applies to all of the other fantastic ideas that come to you, so be sure to act on them as soon as possible and begin with the work that will enable you to be the most productive.

Which one of the following, if you could only do a one activity today, would have the most impact or get you the closest to attaining your objectives?

You may eat that frog.

Who or what is your frog?

What is the one duty that you detest doing yet that must be accomplished?

What activity will get you closer to the overall success and more quickly?

Once you've decided on your "frog," make it a routine to do that chore first thing each morning. To put it another way: devour that frog!

I've created straightforward techniques that make it simpler to recognize and consume your frog. Download my free Eat That Frog guide to start making the most of your time and effort.

Never forget that it is irrelevant where you are coming from. The destination is the only thing that counts!